THE AMERICAN CIVIL WAR

★ THE RIGHT ANSWER ★

THE HOME FRONT

Tim Cooke

Gareth Stevens
Publishing

Please visit our website, www.garethstevens.com. For a free color catalog of all our high-quality books, call toll free 1-800-542-2595 or fax 1-877-542-2596.

Library of Congress Cataloging-in-Publication Data

Cooke, Tim, 1961-
 The home front / Tim Cooke.
     p. cm. — (The American Civil War: the right answer)
 Includes index.
 ISBN 978-1-4339-7544-8 (pbk.)
 ISBN 978-1-4339-7545-5 (6-pack)
 ISBN 978-1-4339-7543-1 (library binding)
 1. United States—History—Civil War, 1861-1865—Social aspects—Juvenile literature. 2. Confederate States of America—Social conditions—Juvenile literature. I. Title.
 E468.9.C66 2012
 973.7'1—dc23

                                              2012013936

Published in 2013 by
Gareth Stevens Publishing
111 East 14th Street, Suite 349
New York, NY 10003

© 2013 Brown Bear Books Ltd.

For Brown Bear Books Ltd:
Editorial Director: Lindsey Lowe
Managing Editor: Tim Cooke
Children's Publisher: Anne O'Daly
Art Director: Jeni Child
Designer: Karen Perry
Picture Manager: Sophie Mortimer
Production Director: Alastair Gourlay

Picture Credits:
Front Cover: Library of Congress

Interior: all images Library of Congress except, Corbis: 5; National Archives: 21, 33; Robert Hunt Library: 6.

All Artworks © Brown Bear Books Ltd.

Manufactured in the United States of America
1 2 3 4 5 6 7 8 9   12 11 10

CPSIA compliance information: Batch #BRS12GS: For further information contact Gareth Stevens, New York, New York at 1-800-542-2595.

Contents

Introduction

The large numbers of troops involved in the Civil War, and the need to keep them supplied, meant that the home front was vitally important to the war effort in both the North and the South.

The Civil War had an impact on the lives of virtually every American. The impact was greater in the South, which was disrupted by fighting and by shortages of food and other commodities, but in the North, the economy was also reshaped to meet the needs of the war. The absence of large numbers of men who joined the armies created a labor shortage. Many vacant jobs were filled by women, who worked outside the home for the first time. Such a change would have a lasting effect on U.S. society.

There were other changes, too. The war had an impact on farming, education, fashion, homes—virtually every aspect of American life. But whatever the changes, they tended to be more dramatic in the South than in either the North or the West. Far more Northerners were able to live in ways that closely resembled their lives before the war. Some Northern cities enjoyed a boom sparked by producing supplies for the war effort. In the South, cities were overcrowded with refugees from the fighting on Southern soil.

About this book

This book describes the impact of the war on the home front in the North and the South, in cities and in the country. The articles are arranged in alphabetical order to make it easy to find information. There are boxes in the margins to help you get more out of your reading. **Comment** boxes highlight pieces of information and explain their importance. **Ask Yourself** boxes suggest questions for you to consider. Other boxes explain difficult words or ideas. The book finishes with a glossary and a list of resources for further information. There is also an index that you can use to follow a particular theme or story through the book.

↻ *A band plays in Philadelphia as part of a drive to recruit volunteers for the Union armies. Hundreds of thousands of men enlisted on both sides, which had a profound impact on the home front.*

Costume and dress

The Civil War changed how civilians dressed. In the Confederacy, fabric shortages meant women learned how to make clothes from drapes, to spin cotton, and to make their own dyes.

🎧 *Mary Todd Lincoln, the wife of President Lincoln, wears a full silk crinoline in this picture from 1861.*

T he clothes people wore at the start of the Civil War showed their social class and wealth. Working people wore clothes that lasted and were practical. Only wealthy people could afford to wear the fashions of the day.

Women's clothes

All women wore lots of layers: underclothes, a corset, a dress with fitted bodice, and a cape. The fashionable dress of the day was the crinoline—a full skirt over a hooped wire frame. Women usually wore a bonnet to cover their hair when they left the home. Wealthy women changed their clothes to suit the time of day and the social occasion.

Women of all classes learned to sew, knit, and embroider. Magazines published the latest fashions from Paris and London for readers to either make or have made.

Children's clothes

Both boys and girls dressed the same—they both wore petticoats—until the age of five. Older boys wore short or long trousers or knickerbockers (baggy trousers gathered below the knee) while girls wore dresses. Seams were let out as the child grew. Clothes were not washed often, so girls wore aprons or pinafores over their dresses to keep them clean. All clothing was fastened by buttons, as the zipper had not yet been invented.

All clothes had been sewn and mended by hand until the sewing machine became widely used in the 1850s.

Men's clothes

During the Civil War, men made their clothes last. They wore dark-colored jackets made of hard-wearing fabrics such as wool. Wealthier men might wear silk or linen.

Men always wore a vest and jacket and were never seen in public wearing just a shirt. The sack coat was popular outerwear during the war. It was less shaped and looser than the more formal shawl-collared jacket. Both working men and the merchant classes wore the sack coat, but the merchants' coats were made of better quality cloth.

↻ *A sketch of the popular men's coat of the Civil War, known as the sack coat.*

⟳ Ulysses S. Grant's family photographed after the war. The girl at the front wears a pinafore and a scholar hat.

Shortages and price rises

Although the North no longer had access to cotton or cloth from the South, Northern women were not as affected by the lack of fabric as women in the South. Southern women spun their own yarn to weave clothes, and dyed and recycled fabric. Before the war, only black slaves and poor whites wore homespun fabric.

In the North, wives and daughters of merchants who had become rich supplying the war effort could buy the latest fashions. Southern women had to rely on Union troops to learn about the latest fashions. The price of cloth in the Confederacy became unaffordable.

Making do

Women in the South used tablecloths and bed linens to make clothes and made their own dyes from berries and roots. They made shoes out of cloth and paper, and their children went barefoot. Some women had to ask their slaves to give back hand-me-downs.

Southern women of all classes were forced to think of inventive ways to dress themselves and their families as the war continued.

⊂ *The actress Pauline Cushman was a Union spy. She is shown here wearing a half-size crinoline with a buttoned-up bodice.*

ASK YOURSELF

How do you think fashionable women would have felt about having to wear the same rough clothes as poorer people?

THE RIGHT ANSWER

?

During the war, women had to worry about feeding their families. Why did they worry about clothes?

For wealthy women in both the North and the South, clothes were an important way in which they told the world about themselves. Clothes were a sign of social status, so keeping up with the latest fashions and fabrics marked women as being wealthy. In the South, especially, women were expected to behave in a certain way. Clothes were another sign of their genteel behavior that they tried to maintain for as long as possible. For men and children, clothes were more practical, and so neither group was as affected by shortages as women were.

Daily life

In the 1860s in the United States, it was where people lived—as well as whether they were male or female, black or white, urban or rural—that determined what kind of life they had.

Where people lived—whether it was the North or the South, or to a lesser extent the West—had the single biggest effect on shaping their daily lives.

Northern life

Most of the 22 million Northerners lived on farms and in small towns, but an increasing number were moving to cities and towns. Boys went to school during the day. If girls went to school, they studied before or after the boys, early in the morning or late in the afternoon.

In urban areas, a child from a wealthy family would attend school all day. At home, he or she might read, play music, or listen to stories. Children had a bath on Saturday nights and went to church on Sundays.

↻ *Inventions such as the home washer and the cookstove saved women time on their household chores.*

HOME WASHING MACHINE & WRINGER.

HOME WASHER

DEPOT 24 CORTLANDT ST., NEW YORK.
DEPOT, 13 BARCLAY ST., NEW YORK.

⊙ **Three young Northern women pose in front of the Union flag. For them, life throughout the war would have carried on much as it had before the war.**

In rural areas, life was harder. There were few schools. Children were taught to read and write at home, but there was little time for learning. Most farming families worked all day.

Southern life

In the South, few children were educated in schools. Plantation owners hired a tutor for their children, and farmers' children might join them. Girls learned useful skills such as sewing. Poorer children worked with their parents on the farm. Black children were not educated at all. By 1860, it was illegal to teach slaves to read and write.

The biggest difference between life in the North and the South was slavery. If you were black in the South, you were probably a slave. There were some free blacks, who worked as laundresses or the black community's ministers, but not many.

> Farm work traditionally began at dawn and lasted to dusk. Once darkness fell, people often went to bed.

> **ASK YOURSELF**
>
> Why do you think slave owners were so eager to prevent slaves from learning to read and write?

Go West!

The West was more socially mobile than either the North or the South. Pioneers on the frontier had little time for social niceties. Life was too hard to keep up differences of status. Most westerners were farmers who settled on lands taken from Native Americans. Some westerners still lived under threat of being attacked, but, by the 1860s, most Native Americans had been pushed so far west that fewer attacks occurred.

➲ *This scene shows a hospital in Washington, D.C. Supplying the armies and looking after the wounded had an increasing effect on daily life as the war went on.*

Hard life

Farming western soil was hard. The weather was tough. Farmers faced tornadoes, baking summer heat, and harsh winters. Small towns grew very slowly, so homes were usually quite remote. Life was often lonely, particularly for women. Western women did the same chores as other women, but without the aid of modern inventions like a cookstove or a sewing machine, or even a hand pump to get water from the well. The divisions of labor between men and women could not survive in such a demanding world as the West. Both men and women worked on the farm or in the business and in the home as was necessary.

The invention of John Deere's steel-bladed plow in 1837 made it easier to prepare soil for planting.

ASK YOURSELF

Were western women forerunners of the movement for equality for women? They did jobs that most Southern and Northern women would not do.

THE RIGHT ANSWER

?

If you had to choose one region to live in during the Civil War, which would you choose?

The answer would likely depend on the color of your skin and your gender. For black Americans, the North was a far more welcoming environment than the South, where most blacks were slaves. For women, the newly expanding West was a tough environment where women had to work as hard as men. In the South, rich women saw their role as one of decoration and maintaining good manners, while poorer women had always worked. In the North, women were increasingly entering the workplace. They could get jobs as teachers and nurses.

Family life

The Civil War has been called the "Brothers' War." Most American families were affected as more men were killed in the fighting. Some families fell out over their support for one side or the other.

T he Civil War changed family life. Domestic life was disrupted as men went off to fight, and women and children were left to fend alone at home.

The Civil War was fought in people's backyards. Some men found themselves fighting in the same fields and orchards they had played in as children. Many civilians lived close to the front lines. Their homes were used as temporary supply bases or even military headquarters; churches and schoolhouses became makeshift hospitals and morgues.

↻ *This etching shows a wounded soldier coming home after the war. Life was greatly changed by injury, death, and other hardships of the war.*

The changing role of women

In the mid-19th century, women's lives centered on the home and family. Only 25 percent of white women worked outside the home before they married, and only 5 percent after marriage.

At the start of the war, women on both sides sewed uniforms, prepared food, and treated minor injuries. Increasingly, women took on responsibilities for which they had little or no practical experience. They ran their husbands' farms and businesses. They worked as farmers, plantation managers, clerks, and munitions-plant workers. Many women became schoolteachers. In North Carolina, by 1865, women made up more than half the staff of the state's schools; in 1860, the proportion had been just 7 percent.

Boys who were too young to enlist took over jobs at home like chopping wood and mending fences. Girls helped their mothers in the kitchen.

Split loyalties

More than 620,000 soldiers and many civilians died in the Civil War. In the South, almost every family was affected by the loss of one or more members.

Families often disagreed on which side to support. President Lincoln's wife's four brothers fought on the Confederate side. One was killed.

ASK YOURSELF

How do you think men returning from the war might feel about their wives' and daughters' new jobs?

↩ *A Union soldier on the battlefield dreams of the day he will be reunited with his family.*

In the North, the army commanders did not have to make such stark choices; they were already in the Union army.

Divided loyalties

General Robert E. Lee was forced to make a difficult choice between his conscience on one hand and his family and career on the other. He was the son of "Lighthorse" Harry Lee, a hero of the Revolutionary War (1775–1783), and had served in the U.S. Army for 30 years. But when Winfield Scott, Lincoln's general in chief, offered Lee command of the Union forces, Lee declined. He could not fight against his native Virginia. As he said: "I could not raise my hand against my birthplace, my home, my children." Lee resigned his commission and later became commander of the Confederate Army of Northern Virginia. It would be the most famous of the Confederate armies, which Lee led with distinction.

Many other individuals had to make difficult choices. Flora Cook was the daughter of General St. George Cook of the Union army and wife of J.E.B. ("Jeb") Stuart. Jeb resigned his commission in the U.S. Army to join the Confederacy. At the outbreak of the war, he asked Flora to move with him and their children to the Confederacy. Although her Unionist family was shocked, Flora resettled with her husband in Saltville, Virginia.

The Civil War damaged families in many ways. It was not just that many men died and left households incomplete. The war also caused crises of conscience and principle that were impossible to settle without great family pain.

ASK YOURSELF

Do you think that your family would have all taken the same side in the Civil War? Do you always agree about everything?

THE RIGHT ANSWER

?

How did the Civil War's profound effect continue to influence families after the war?

Few families escaped the pain and suffering of the Civil War. In the South, most families lost a husband, father, brother, or son. In the North, casualties were not as high, but families still suffered. In the South, families experienced the horror of war at close hand as battles were fought next to their homes. But, alongside the deaths, life-changing injuries, and long absences, there were further family conflicts. Some families split over which side to support during the war. Their differences were often so bitter that they could not be put aside once the war was over.

Food and drink

At the start of the war, the United States was a farming economy that could feed all its citizens. During the war, that was no longer true of the South. High prices and shortages were common.

Feeding their soldiers a basic food ration of hardtack, beef, beans, and coffee was the responsibility of both armies. Union rations changed little during the war, but in the South, rations were reduced as the war went on.

Hardtack was a soldier's staple food. It was useful because it didn't spoil and was fairly nutrious. Made from flour, salt, and water, it was like a dry cracker. In the South, it was often made from cornmeal. Hardtack was made behind the lines and shipped in barrels to the camps.

↺ *A cartoon in Harper's Weekly of June 1, 1861, shows a butcher, followed by rows of "volunteer" chefs, cattle, pigs, and sauce bottles.*

⊖ *Hungry residents of New Orleans fight to get bread handed out by the authorities after the Union occupation of the city.*

Meats such as pork and salted beef were also staples. Beef was a common food, and cattle were sometimes driven along with troops on the march and then slaughtered as required. Eating bad meat often made soldiers sick and even killed some. Beans were used a lot, as they added bulk to meals and were cheap.

Families sometimes sent food parcels to the soldiers, who could also buy food from sutlers. These licensed traders sold provisions such as pickles, cheese, and candies, as well as liquor, from their wagons. Often this food was prepared in unhygenic conditions and made soldiers sick. Foraging, or gathering food from the countryside, was another way to supplement rations.

Bacon grease was used to soak hardtack to make it taste better.

ASK YOURSELF

Should soldiers have had to pay for their own food while they were away fighting in the army?

Confederate home front

Prices in the South rose from 1861 as farmers hoarded crops and the Union blockade took effect. By 1863, many Southerners were hungry

ASK YOURSELF

Do you think that the Confederate government had a responsibility to ensure everyone had food?

and desperate for basic foods. In April, an angry mob rioted in Richmond, Virginia, demanding that the government hand out bread.

By early 1863, meat rarely featured in the daily diet across the South. Many families were reduced to a diet of cornbread supplemented by sorghum, field peas, and milk. Every social class of Southerners ate cornbread.

Farmers and other families who lived in the country and could grow their own food usually had better food to eat than those who lived in towns and had to buy their food. Food had become very expensive. Rapid inflation meant that, by mid-1863, Southerners paid $50 or more a bushel for corn. Prices were even higher for people living close to the front lines or in towns.

Buying goods

Coffee was a popular drink. The North bought the best possible coffee for its troops. In the South, coffee was a mainstay of the whole way of life.

↻ *Confederate raiders steal Union cattle in this sketch by Alfred Waud.*

However, the Union blockade meant that both civilians and soldiers had to make do with coffee substitutes, such as acorn or cotton coffee. One possible source of coffee beans was the Northern peddlers who traveled south with laden wagons, but loyal Southerners did not want to buy from the enemy. In addition, inflation meant that few of them could afford the peddlers' prices.

⊙ *This label for "hygienic" whiskey dates from 1860. Alcohol was used to clean wounds to help stop infection.*

ASK YOURSELF

If your family was hungry and you could afford the peddlers' high prices, do you think you would have bought food from them?

THE RIGHT ANSWER

?

During the war, you would have eaten much better in the North than the South. Why?

Across the South, the Union blockade cut off food supplies. As the South's transportation network broke down, it was hard to get even the food that was still being grown to the people who needed it. In the North, on the other hand, food crops were harvested and distributed as normal. New inventions like the tin can and condensed milk meant that Union troops could get a wider range of supplies. Some Union soldiers ate better than they ever had. In the South, civilians and, later, troops went hungry. Children were often malnourished and underweight.

Home front, Confederacy

The impact of the war affected civilians in the South far more than those in the North. Shortages of food together with the frequency of fighting on Southern soil brought widespread suffering.

Unlike their Northern counterparts, most Southerners welcomed the war when it began in 1861. They thought that the conflict would be short and the North quickly defeated.

A popular cause?

The elite planter class led support for the Confederate cause and never lost it. They assumed that everyone else had the same hope for a Southern victory, even their slaves. When some poorer white men were reluctant to join the army, this elite thought it was due to personal cowardice rather than political belief.

With so many men away fighting, women ran family estates and farms. They often found it difficult to manage slaves with the same authority as men, however. Slaves started to ignore orders or run away

◑ *Confederates evacuate Brownsville, Texas, in 1864. The town was an important trade route for goods from across the border with Mexico.*

to join the Union army. Still, many of the planter class of women found it difficult to grasp that slavery might be ending.

Women of poorer families labored in the fields while their husbands were in the army. They resented legislation such as the Twenty Negro Law, which they felt favored the upper classes.

Shortages bite

By 1862, food shortages were severe in the South. The problem was often not a lack of food but lack of a way to distribute it. Military shipments took priority on poor transportation systems, so food rotted away in warehouses. The Union blockade was also very effective. It made it almost impossible to get everyday goods such as cloth, leather shoes, and coffee. The shortages were made worse by high inflation. The prices of some goods rose more than sevenfold. Even basic foods became unaffordable for most people.

The Confederacy's "Twenty Negro Law" allowed white men with more than 20 slaves to avoid military service.

ASK YOURSELF

Why do you think the military had priority in transportation? Should the government have changed this?

Life for refugees

At least 250,000 Southerners became refugees. Most fled to cities such as Richmond, Columbia, and Atlanta.

As the war went on, life was usually more difficult in the overcrowded cities of the South than the countryside. Food was scarcer, for one thing. But many rural families fled to the cities because their homes and farms lay in the path of invading troops. A month into the war, northern Virginians started to leave their homes; by 1862, the number had dramatically increased.

Large numbers of people fleeing from an invading army often caused chaos. At the end of 1864, Union general William T. Sherman's troops marched through Georgia and the Carolinas, destroying everything in their path and causing yet more families to flee. The impact on Columbia, South Carolina, was immediate. The prewar population of 8,000 rose to 24,000 by

⟲ *The Tredegar Iron Works in Richmond, Virginia, was the only ironworks in the whole of the South at the start of the war.*

February 1865. When Sherman's arrival was imminent, officials, military personnel, and civilians all rushed to leave at the same time. Trains were overloaded as people flocked to the station to try to escape before Sherman arrived.

As any hope of a Confederate win disappeared, bitterness grew in its place. The legend of a Lost Cause took hold during the Reconstruction era as the defeated Confederates struggled to rebuild their lives in the devastated Southern states.

COMMENT

The Lost Cause was an idea that the old Southern way of life was ideal, but it had been savagely destroyed by the aggression of those in the North.

THE RIGHT ANSWER

?

Some Southerners welcomed the end of the war while others did not. Why was that?

The devastation caused by Sherman's "March to the Sea" was the final straw for many Southerners. The countryside had been destroyed. The South had little infrastructure left. Poorer Southerners had long suffered from shortages and upheaval; they were more eager for the war to end than to fight for the Confederate cause. Among the planter class, where suffering had not usually been so bad, many wanted the war to continue. But defeat was virtually inevitable; so many soldiers had deserted there was no longer a credible army to fight. Surrender was the only choice.

Home front, Union

Civilian life in the Union continued during the war much as before. Food shortages were not too severe, and the much-hated draft did not affect the Union population as much as it did the Confederacy.

⌕ **This fair was held in 1864 by the U.S. Sanitary Commission in a Brooklyn theater to raise money to support Union soldiers.**

Civilian life in the Union was much better than life in the Confederacy throughout the entire war.

Life in the Union

The Union had several advantages over the South. Its population was more than four times larger, and it had far more resources. The North's economy was based on industry and manufacturing; the Southern economy was wholly based on agriculture.

In order to fight a war, however, the North still had to meet basic requirements. It needed volunteers to serve in the army, a supportive civilian population, and strong, organized leaders. None of these things happened automatically. To fill its army, the federal government assigned each state a quota of troops and then waited for them to enlist the required number of soldiers.

While many men enlisted, the people who stayed at home supported the war effort by keeping the economy going. Men managed farms or worked in industries. Women started to work as laborers. Later, they also became government clerks or nurses as need overcame prewar prejudices against women in the workplace.

The Union raised more than two million men for military service, including more than 180,000 African Americans; most of these men were volunteers.

Unrest and patriotism

Wartime inflation meant that prices rose faster than wages. Some workers went on strike in protest, but the strikes rarely succeeded. The army was sometimes called in to force strikers back to work. The Union introduced the draft in March 1863. That July in New York City, a mob protesting the draft attacked draft offices and killed free blacks, whom they blamed for the war and for conscription. At least 105 people died. The draft riot was an extreme example of the opposition felt by many in the Union toward the

◔ *Volunteers in Philadelphia ran this hospital for injured soldiers.*

This bedroom shows the simple kind of furniture people had in their homes during the war.

way the war was being fought. The Democratic Party, however, which was the main political opposition to the government, was split in its views on the war and did not have a united voice.

Voluntary organizations

Patriotic civilians formed organizations to raise money and collect supplies for the war. The Soldiers' Aid Associations and the U.S. Sanitary Commission raised funds and were helped by volunteers. Sanitary fairs were held in large Northern cities and raised millions of dollars.

The U.S. Sanitary Commission was set up in 1861 to provide improved hygiene and medical care for troops in the field.

Border life

In the Union border states, the war had a direct impact on civilian life. Kentucky tried to remain neutral in the conflict but was invaded by both

Confederate and Union troops. It was probably the most divided state in the war; many families were split by their loyalties. In Maryland, the Union government treated the supporters of secession harshly. It kept parts of the state under occupation, controlled state elections, and imprisoned civilians without trial. Missouri was another border state to suffer. Some 1,162 battles and skirmishes took place on its soil (only Virginia and Tennessee had more fighting), as its civilians were terrorized by pro-Union and pro-Confederate guerrilla bands.

⊙ *This factory on the East River in New York made iron items such as gates and railings; the North had far more industry than the South.*

THE RIGHT ANSWER

?

What was the impact of the Civil War on civilian life in the Union once it ended?

The Civil War continued to shape daily life long after 1865. The federal government was far more powerful than at the start of the war, and its power grew more during Reconstruction (1865–1877). Women who had begun to work outside the home continued to do so. Although their position in society had improved, however, it would still be another 50 years before women won the right to vote. The contribution of African Americans to the Union victory changed their place in Northern society; but again, it was many years before black Americans were to gain equality.

Homes and furniture

Dark, ornate furniture and richly colored fabrics were fashionable during the Civil War. The style was known as "Victorian" for Queen Victoria, who ruled Great Britain between 1837 and 1901.

⌂ *This manor house stands at Shirley Plantation, the oldest plantation in Virginia.*

I n the 1860s, the fashion was for large houses, with painted gables and porches on the outside and interiors that were cluttered with furniture.

By the mid-19th century, more Americans had become part of the middle class. They had left their family farms to work in towns and cities. They wanted homes and furnishings to match their new status.

A wealthy Northern city dweller might live in a two-story stone house. The less well-off tended to move to the new suburbs, where houses were cheaper. Poor families could only afford to rent a small apartment in a tenement building shared with other families.

The Southern centers of commerce, such as Savannah, Charleston, and Richmond, had many stylish houses for the business classes. But most of the South was rural and had very different architecture. Farmers might live in simple wood-frame houses. Such homes had little in common with either the huts of slaves or the elegant plantation houses of the wealthy elite.

Different styles

The wealthy built homes in a variety of styles from Europe, such as the Italianate style. But an American style was emerging, and architecture was just starting as a profession. Some architects published their plans; builders copied them for rich clients in other parts of the country.

People built homes with whatever materials were close at hand; they built log cabins where wood was plentiful and adobe brick homes in the desert.

ASK YOURSELF

Why do you think American styles of building might have started to appear?

⊖ *This drawing shows a tenement block on the Lower East Side, Manhattan, in 1873; living conditions in such blocks were often unhealthy.*

➔ *Abraham Lincoln bought this house in Springfield, Illinois, in 1844. He lived there for 17 years before he became U.S. president.*

To keep homes cool, houses were built with high ceilings so the air would circulate and with overhanging porches to keep out the sunlight.

Interiors

A house's external appearance said a lot about the status and wealth of the family who lived there. In the same way, the rooms where people met visitors—known as reception rooms—also conveyed a message about the inhabitants. Middle-class women were responsible for creating spaces that were comfortable but also showed the family's accomplishments. Interior decoration became important, and women turned to magazines and books for advice on colors, furniture, lighting, and wallpapers.

Modern technology

There was no central heating or electricity. Rooms were heated by open fires and lit by candles or kerosene lamps. Piped gas was just being introduced to cities, so a few homes had gas lighting. Very few homes had running water. Water was drawn by hand, and chamber pots and outhouses were used instead of flush toilets. At all levels of society, people bathed infrequently.

Furniture

Furniture was often handed down through the family. Increasingly, people also bought new items from local cabinetmakers or from manufacturers in the big cities. New furniture was often based on old styles, such as Gothic or rococo. Rooms were stuffed full with parlor suites, writing bureaus, tables, chairs, and coatracks.

⟳ Stratford Hall, Virginia, was the boyhood home of Robert E. Lee. It was built by his great-grandfather, Thomas Lee, in the 1730s.

THE RIGHT ANSWER

?

Americans have always loved their homes and taken pride in them. Did this start in the Civil War?

The Civil War coincided with the start of industrialization and an economic boom that would bring decades of prosperity to the United States. Despite the devastating effects of the war and the destruction it caused, many Americans were already changing how they lived. In the North, the new middle classes were settling in cities, where they bought new houses. They furnished their homes to reflect their personalities and aspirations. In the South, most people still lived in the countryside. Homes there tended to directly reflect the wealth of their owners.

Rural life

Working the land was tough in the 19th century. Workers toiled by hand, but the Civil War coincided with the start of an agricultural revolution. Machines began to do much of the work.

⟳ *Slaves stack wheat by hand in fields in Virginia in this drawing from 1863.*

At the start of the Civil War, there were two million farms in the United States. More than half of the labor force worked on farms or in trades directly related to agriculture. Farm life had been improved by advances such as kerosene lamps, which brought better lighting to rural homes. The growing railroad network also created new markets for farm produce.

The Civil War brought high crop prices and a shortage of workers. Farmers in the North started to use mechanized equipment to meet the needs of increased production.

↷ *A sketch published in Harper's Weekly on March 26, 1864, shows slaves leaving a Southern farm on horseback to join Union forces.*

The reaper

By the start of the war, around 70 percent of the wheat raised west of the Appalachian Mountains was being harvested using machines. Labor shortages encouraged grain farmers to use improved reapers. In 1865, for example, the McCormick Company sold 7,000 reapers. When the war began, reapers had a crew of eight to ten men, who harvested 10–12 acres (4–4.8 ha) per day. By the end of the war, improvements meant that eight men harvested 15 acres (6 ha) per day.

Other inventions

Along with the reaper, other improved implements were also introduced, such as grain drills, horse-powered threshing machines, and riding plows. These new tools reduced the worker-hours required to produce 1 acre (0.4 ha)

The mechanical reaper had been developed in 1833 to cut down grain in the fields. Previously, it had been done by hand and was very time consuming.

ASK YOURSELF

How did farmers afford these machines? Did they share the cost or did they rent them? Or both?

of wheat from 35 to 20. Such changes meant that Northern farmers could not only feed their civilians and soldiers but could even export food. New canning technology improved the preservation of fruits and vegetables. Another invention was condensed milk. Gail Borden's new method of preserving and canning milk provided a new market for dairy farmers and improved nutrition for Union soldiers.

Southern rural life

Few agricultural advances made it to the South. The Confederate government told manufacturers to make weapons, not agricultural tools. Cotton still had to be picked by hand because no one had yet developed a mechanical harvester. Many

⟳ *This advertisement for agricultural machinery shows various ways in which new inventions could be used.*

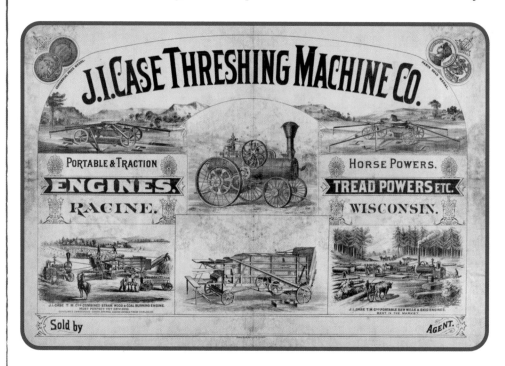

plantation owners would not use the new tools. They argued that mechanization would decrease the need for slave labor and so reduce the value of their investment. This showed their inability to understand that slavery was on its way out.

Replacement parts and new tools became increasingly scarce in the South during the war. As equipment wore out or was destroyed in fighting, it could not be replaced.

Iron goods were scarce through the South, where most iron was used for the war effort.

THE RIGHT ANSWER

?

Why was there such a big difference between agriculture in the North and the South?

During the Civil War, Northern farmers increased their food production. With the help of new and improved agricultural technology, they were able to feed the domestic market and export food. In the South, farmers struggled to feed their soldiers and civilians. They had concentrated too much on labor-intensive cotton production. When the war ended, the North's farms were in good shape; they had become part of the market economy. In the South, the farmers and planters had lost their slave workers and also lacked modern agricultural machinery.

Schools and education

Americans were some of the best educated people in the world at the start of the war. Literacy rates were highest in New England, where they reached 90 percent among adults.

○ **This drawing shows cadets at the Citadel, a military academy in Charleston, South Carolina, where students learned military drill and tactics as part of their basic education.**

Public education had been set up in Northern states in the 1830s. There was a mixture of public, private, charity, and Christian schools. Rural children attended one-room schoolhouses or were educated at home.

Southern attitudes

In the South, less emphasis was placed on education: only 80 percent of the white population was literate. Children tended to have to work with their parents in the fields to plant and harvest the crops, so only one-third of white Southern children enrolled in school. Even those who did enroll only went to school for an average of three months a year.

Many Southerners were wary of education. They saw it as a "Yankee" idea from the industrialized North that had no place in an agricultural society. A South Carolina newspaper said, "To make every child in the state a literary character would not be a good qualification for those who must live by manual labor."

Different attitudes

Apart from in Massachusetts, white and black children in the North were educated separately. Black schools often had to rely on charitable donations, as it was difficult to get enough funding from local school boards that were controlled by whites. Black schools often lacked even basics like heating, furniture, and books. Some "Negro colleges" existed in the Northern states to educate free blacks. Most were privately funded, like Avery College in Pittsburgh, which the abolitionist Charles Avery started in 1849 with a fund of $300,000.

In New York, the Manumission Society paid for special "Negro schools," but it was the exception rather than the rule.

◔ *Mount St. Mary's College in Emmitsburg, Maryland, is the oldest Catholic educational establishment in the United States; it was founded in 1808.*

 ➲ *John Clem was only 10 years old when he ran away from home to become a drummer boy in the Union army; he later became a noted U.S. Army general.*

Rhode Island desegregated its schools in 1865. In 1867, Connecticut followed suit and educated black and white kids together.

Attitudes start to change

As attitudes toward Northern blacks altered during the war, many states started to increase funding for black education. After the war, voluntary organizations in the South offered a form of education to freed slaves. Many Negro schools were run by the Freedman's Aid organizations. In the postwar era, Southern education remained segregated, however. Funding for black schools was usually far less than that for white schools.

Forging an identity

Religion, particularly the values of Protestant Christianity, was a key part of education in the Northern states. Students also learned about the U.S. government. They had to memorize the federal catechism (a series of questions and answers about the Constitution) from Webster's *American Spelling Book*.

In the South, schoolbooks emphasized the rights of the Confederate cause over the Yankees' wrongdoing. Children were encouraged to see themselves as the next Confederate generation. School classrooms in both the North and South created strong patriotic identities.

Students studied the *New England Primer*, which included phrases like "In Adam's Fall, we sinned all."

ASK YOURSELF

Do you think textbooks should try to promote a political view? Does that sort of thing happen today?

THE RIGHT ANSWER

?

What were the main differences in the impact of the war on education in the North and in the South?

In the North, the war had little direct impact. Some older pupils left school to work in place of their absent fathers. When many male teachers went away to fight, women became teachers in large numbers. In the South, the impact was far greater. Fewer children went to school, as parents could no longer afford to send them or needed them to work. Many teachers enlisted, although they were exempt from the draft, as did older boys. Falling enrollments forced some schools to close. Often, schools that lost high numbers of teachers or pupils as casualties never reopened.

Urban life

During the war, most civilians tried to live as normally as possible. Whether they were able to achieve this depended on where they lived and whether they were in the Union or Confederacy.

I n 1860, one-quarter of all Northerners lived in towns and cities. Only Washington, D.C., and Philadelphia were directly affected by the war. In cities such as New York, Boston, and Chicago, the war often seemed a long way away.

In the South, only one-tenth of the population lived in urban areas. In the Confederate capital, Richmond, war was always close by. Cities such as Nashville, Vicksburg, and New Orleans were under Union occupation by 1863.

◡ *People ice-skate at a winter carnival held in Brooklyn, New York City, on February 10, 1862.*

Problems in New York

Northern cities also had their problems, however. In July 1863, a riot broke out in New York City against the draft. Rioters killed more than a hundred people as the police lost control. The situation was inflamed by long-standing racial tensions. Irish immigrants made up 25 percent of the city's 800,000 residents. They were mostly uneducated and unskilled. They lived in slums in lower Manhattan and competed for the same menial jobs as poor blacks.

The Irish picked on blacks, whom they saw as their inferiors. Like other poor Northerners, they felt the draft was unfair. People with money were able to avoid the draft by hiring a substitute to take their place or by paying an exemption fee.

A few Northerners who were involved in war contracts actually experienced a new period of economic prosperity.

ASK YOURSELF

Do you think it was fair that the better-off could buy their way out of military service?

From the First Battle of Bull Run in July 1861 until July 1864, Washington was prepared for imminent invasion by the South.

Life in Washington

In Washington, D.C., war was just around the corner. The city became a military encampment. There were soldiers everywhere, and the Mall was lined with temporary field hospitals. But the city was built on swampy land, and its environment was not healthy for the sick and wounded. Disease was everywhere, and many men died not from their wounds but from sickness.

Southern life

Life in Southern cities was hard. The Union blockade and rampant inflation meant that living standards fell dramatically. Women took on the work of men who were away fighting. Ladies could no longer buy fine clothes. It took all their energies to find food for the table. Despite the fact that they had such a hard

◔ *Wall Street, New York, as it looked in 1847. The narrow Manhattan street was the financial capital of the nation.*

time, Confederate city dwellers accepted that sacrifices were necessary for the war effort. This compared starkly with the Union, where many people were either indifferent to the war or actually against it.

The worst outbreak of discontent in the Confederacy took place in April 1863. A mob of mainly women went on the rampage in Richmond demanding bread. Starving women looted bakeries and food stores, and also stole clothing and jewelry.

⌒ *This view of Washington, D.C., in May 1865 includes the Capitol in the distance.*

THE RIGHT ANSWER

?

Life was much harder for those living in Southern rather than Northern cities; why was that?

The war played out across the South. There was fighting close to the capital of Richmond and in Nashville, New Orleans, and Vicksburg. People had to get used to food and clothing shortages as the Union blockade took control. Inflation meant they could no longer live well. People were starving. In the North, the citizens of Washington, D.C., were far more aware of the horrors of war than in cities such as Boston, which was geographically a long way from the fighting. In New York, the war increased tensions that already divided different groups and classes.

Glossary

blockade: Measures designed to prevent a country trading by blocking access to or from its ports.

catechism: A type of learning by rote, usually through a repeated series of questions and answers.

draft: The compulsory recruitment of men to serve in the armed forces.

federal: Related to the national government based in Washington, D.C.

guerrillas: Irregular soldiers who fought by methods such as ambushes and raids.

hardtack: A type of dry cracker that was the standard food for soldiers on both sides.

homespun: A rough cloth that is woven from yarn made at home.

inflation: A general rise in prices.

peddler: A trader who travels around, selling goods from a wagon.

pioneer: A settler who went to live on the American frontier in the 19th century.

plantation: A large argicultural estate; in the South, plantations were used for growing crops such as cotton.

rations: A limited amount of food to which an individual is entitled during times of shortage.

reaper: A machine used for harvesting wheat or corn.

refugee: Someone who has to leave his or her home for safety, usually because of warfare or a natural disaster.

sanitary fair: A fund-raising event to help improve conditions for soldiers in camp.

sutlers: Civilian traders who were licensed to supply food to army camps.

territories: Areas of North America that had some elements of government but which had not entered the Union as states.

Further reading

Baxter, Roberta. *The Northern Home Front of the Civil War* (Heinemann Infosearch). Heinemann Raintree, 2010.

Baxter, Roberta. *The Southern Home Front of the Civil War* (Heinemann Infosearch). Heinemann Raintree, 2010.

Kreiser, Lawrence A., and Ray B. Browne. *Voices of Civil War America: Contemporary Accounts of Daily Life* (Voices of an Era). Greenwood, 2011.

Mattern, Joanne. *The Big Book of the Civil War: Fascinating Facts about the Civil War.* Courage Books, 2007.

Robertson, James. *The Untold Civil War: Exploring the Human Side of War.* National Geographic, 2011.

Stanchak, John E. *Civil War* (DK Eyewitness Books). DK Publishing, 2011.

Varhola, Michael J. *Life in Civil War America.* Family Tree Books, 2011.

Websites

History Place interactive timeline of the Civil War
www.historyplace.com/civilwar
Smithsonian Institution page with resources on the Civil War.
http//www.civilwar.si.edu

A site supporting the PBS film *The Civil War*, directed by Ken Burns.
http//www.pbs.org/civilwar

Publisher's note to educators and parents: Our editors have carefully reviewed these websites to ensure that they are suitable for students. Many websites change frequently, however, and we cannot guarantee that a site's future contents will continue to meet our high standards of quality and educational value. Be advised that students should be closely supervised whenever they access the Internet.

Index